HOLIDAY AIR FRYER EXTRAVAGANZA

FESTIVE RECIPES FOR EVERY CELEBRATION

By

BELLA V. HENRY

Copyright © 2024 BELLA V. HENRY

Table of Contents

"INTRODUCTION

Welcome to the "Holiday Air Fryer Extravaganza: Festive Recipes for Every Celebration"! As the holiday season approaches, it's time to elevate your culinary experience with the magic of air frying. In this cookbook, we embark on a flavorful journey, exploring a multitude of recipes designed to make your holidays not only delicious but also stress-free.

In this introduction, we'll delve into the essence of holiday cooking, the rising popularity of air fryers, and how this culinary tool can revolutionize the way you prepare festive meals. Whether you're a seasoned chef or a kitchen novice, the simplicity and versatility of air frying will add a dash of excitement to your holiday celebrations.

Get ready to discover mouthwatering recipes for Thanksgiving, Christmas, Hanukkah, New Year's Eve, Valentine's Day, Easter, Fourth of July, and more. From classic dishes to creative twists, each recipe is tailored to bring joy and flavor to your gatherings.

So, let the holiday festivities begin as we embark on this delicious adventure through the "Holiday Air Fryer Extravaganza," where every celebration becomes a culinary masterpiece. Happy cooking!

CHAPTER 1: GETTING STARTED WITH HOLIDAY AIR FRYER COOKING

1.1 Introduction to Holiday Air Fryer Magic

Explore the convenience and versatility of air fryers during the holiday season.

Highlight how air frying reduces cooking time and enhances flavors.

1.2 Essential Tools and Ingredients

List the must-have tools for successful air frying during the holidays.

Identify key ingredients that will be frequently used in the recipes.

1.3 Navigating Your Air Fryer Settings

Guide readers through understanding and adjusting air fryer temperature and cooking times.

Provide tips on selecting the right settings for different holiday dishes.

1.4 Preparing Your Kitchen for Festive Cooking

Organizational tips for a smooth cooking experience.

Suggestions for planning ahead and preparing ingredients in advance.

1.5 Troubleshooting Tips for Air Fryer Success

Address common issues and challenges users may encounter.

Offer solutions to ensure a seamless cooking experience.

1.6 Safety Reminders and Best Practices

Emphasize safety precautions when using an air fryer.

Highlight best practices to avoid accidents and ensure a enjoyable cooking process.

1.7 Sample Holiday Air Fryer Menu

Present a sample menu to showcase the diversity of dishes covered in the book.

Provide a sneak peek into the exciting recipes that lie ahead.

1.8 Conclusion of Chapter 1

Recap the key points discussed in getting started with holiday air fryer cooking.

Encourage readers to feel confident and excited about exploring the upcoming festive recipes in the following chapters.

Chapter 1 sets the foundation for an enjoyable cooking experience throughout the holiday season, providing readers with the knowledge and confidence to make the most out of their air fryers.

OVERVIEW OF ESSENTIAL TOOLS AND INGREDIENTS.

1.2 Essential Tools and Ingredients:

Tools:

Air Fryer:

Choose a reliable air fryer with adjustable temperature settings and a spacious basket for versatile cooking.

Instant-Read Thermometer:

Ensure precision in cooking temperatures, especially for meats and baked goods.

Oil Mister or Cooking Spray:

Opt for a misting tool to evenly coat food with oil, promoting crispiness in air-fried dishes.

Silicone Tongs or Wooden Utensils:

Use non-scratch tools to avoid damaging the air fryer basket while flipping or removing food.

Baking Pans and Trays:

Select compatible pans and trays for baking and roasting in the air fryer.

Parchment Paper or Perforated Liners:

Line the air fryer basket with parchment paper or perforated liners for easy cleanup and to prevent sticking.

Kitchen Timer:

Keep track of cooking times accurately, ensuring your holiday dishes are perfectly cooked.

Measuring Cups and Spoons:

Measure ingredients precisely for consistent and delicious results.

Ingredients:

Quality Cooking Oil:

Choose oils with high smoke points, such as vegetable, canola, or grapeseed oil, for air frying.

Herbs and Spices:

Build a collection of holiday-inspired herbs and spices to add depth and flavor to your dishes.

Fresh Produce:

Stock up on seasonal fruits and vegetables for vibrant, nutrient-rich additions to your recipes.

Holiday Proteins:

Include a variety of proteins like turkey, ham, shrimp, and chicken for festive main courses.

Dairy and Cheeses:

Incorporate cheeses, butter, and cream for richness in certain holiday recipes.

Flour and Breadcrumbs:

Have all-purpose flour and breadcrumbs on hand for coating and breading air-fried foods.

Sweeteners:

Include sugar, honey, or maple syrup for balancing flavors in both savory and sweet dishes.

Specialty Ingredients:

Explore unique ingredients like cranberries, nuts, or seasonal spices for an extra touch of holiday flair.

Remember to adapt the ingredient list based on the specific recipes in each chapter, and feel free to experiment with variations to suit your taste preferences. Having these essential tools and ingredients in your kitchen will set the stage for a successful and delicious holiday air frying experience.

TIPS FOR CHOOSING THE RIGHT AIR FRYER SETTINGS FOR HOLIDAY RECIPES.

1.3 Navigating Your Air Fryer Settings: Tips for Holiday Recipes

Understand Temperature Variations:

Familiarize yourself with the temperature range of your air fryer. Higher temperatures are suitable for quicker cooking, while lower temperatures can be used for gentle crisping.

Preheat for Optimal Results:

Preheat the air fryer before adding ingredients. This ensures even cooking and helps achieve that coveted crispy texture.

Adjust Cooking Times:

Be mindful of the suggested cooking times in recipes but be ready to adjust based on your air fryer's specific characteristics. Frequent monitoring prevents overcooking.

Rotate or Flip Ingredients:

Some air fryers have uneven heat distribution. To counteract this, rotate or flip ingredients halfway through cooking to achieve uniform crispiness.

Use Accessories Wisely:

Experiment with accessories like racks or skewers that come with your air fryer. They can optimize airflow and help cook multiple items simultaneously.

Master Multi-Level Cooking:

If your air fryer allows it, leverage multi-level cooking by placing different dishes on separate levels. Adjust temperatures and cooking times accordingly.

Employ Pacing Techniques:

When preparing a multi-course holiday meal, plan recipes with varying cooking times. Start with items that take longer and add quicker-cooking items later.

Customize Temperature Combinations:

For recipes involving multiple components, consider customizing temperature settings for each. This allows you to achieve the desired textures for diverse ingredients in one go.

Experiment with Airflow Control:

Some air fryers feature airflow control options. Adjusting this can impact crispiness. Experiment to find the setting that suits your preferences.

Keep It Light:

For delicate items like pastries or desserts, opt for lower temperatures to avoid browning too quickly. Lightly brushing with oil can enhance browning without overheating.

Consider Preparing in Batches:

If cooking large quantities, it might be more efficient to prepare items in batches. This ensures each batch receives proper attention and achieves the desired outcome.

Document Your Success:

Keep a record of successful settings for your favorite holiday recipes. This becomes a valuable reference for future cooking sessions.

Remember, mastering air fryer settings is a learning process. Embrace experimentation and fine-tune settings based on your air fryer's nuances and the specific requirements of each holiday recipe. Happy air frying!

CHAPTER 2: THANKSGIVING DELIGHTS

2.1 Introduction to Thanksgiving Air Fryer Cooking

Explore the significance of Thanksgiving and how air frying can simplify the preparation of classic dishes.

Set the tone for a feast of flavors with air-fried delights.

2.2 Air-Fried Turkey Bites with Herb Marinade

Step-by-step guide to creating succulent turkey bites infused with a savory herb marinade.

Emphasize the time-saving benefits of air frying for Thanksgiving main courses.

2.3 Crispy Sweet Potato Fries with Cinnamon Sugar

Unleash the perfect blend of sweetness and crispiness with air-fried sweet potato fries.

Highlight the healthier alternative to traditional deep-fried options.

2.4 Sage and Sausage Stuffing Balls

Elevate the classic stuffing with the convenience of air frying.

Provide variations for different stuffing preferences, catering to various tastes.

2.5 Cranberry Glazed Brussels Sprouts

Transform Brussels sprouts into a festive side dish with a tangy cranberry glaze.

Emphasize the ease of achieving a caramelized finish with the air fryer.

2.6 Thanksgiving Leftovers Remix: Turkey-Stuffed Empanadas

Showcase a creative way to repurpose Thanksgiving leftovers into flavorful empanadas.

Encourage readers to reduce food waste with this tasty and practical recipe.

2.7 Festive Pumpkin Pie Bites

Introduce a bite-sized version of the classic pumpkin pie, air-fried to perfection.

Share tips on achieving a golden crust and creamy filling in a fraction of the time.

2.8 Turkey Day Tips: Planning and Execution

Provide a Thanksgiving meal planning guide for incorporating air-fried dishes seamlessly.

Offer tips for coordinating cooking times to ensure a well-timed feast.

2.9 Reader Submissions: Share Your Thanksgiving Air Fryer Success

Encourage readers to share their experiences and variations of Thanksgiving recipes.

Highlight a selection of submissions to inspire others and foster a sense of community.

2.10 Conclusion of Chapter 2

Recap the mouthwatering Thanksgiving recipes presented in the chapter.

Invite readers to savor the joy of Thanksgiving with a modern twist, courtesy of the air fryer.

Chapter 2 promises a Thanksgiving feast like never before, blending traditional flavors with the efficiency and convenience of air frying. From succulent turkey bites to sweet potato fries, these air-fried delights are sure to make your Thanksgiving celebration memorable. Happy air frying and happy Thanksgiving!

AIR-FRIED TURKEY BITES WITH HERB MARINADE

Ingredients:

1 pound turkey breast, cut into bite-sized cubes

2 tablespoons olive oil

2 cloves garlic, minced

1 tablespoon fresh rosemary, finely chopped

1 tablespoon fresh thyme, finely chopped

1 tablespoon fresh sage, finely chopped

1 teaspoon dried oregano

1 teaspoon smoked paprika

Salt and black pepper, to taste

Instructions:

Prepare the Marinade:

In a bowl, combine olive oil, minced garlic, chopped rosemary, thyme, sage, oregano, smoked paprika, salt, and black pepper. Mix well to form a herb-infused marinade.

Marinate the Turkey:

Place the turkey cubes in a shallow dish or a resealable plastic bag. Pour the herb marinade over the turkey, ensuring each piece is well coated. Seal the bag or cover the dish and refrigerate for at least 30 minutes to let the flavors meld.

Preheat the Air Fryer:

Preheat your air fryer to 375°F (190°C) for about 5 minutes.

Thread the Turkey Bites:

Remove the marinated turkey from the fridge. Thread the turkey cubes onto skewers, leaving a little space between each piece to ensure even cooking.

Air Fry the Turkey Bites:

Place the skewers in the air fryer basket, ensuring they are not overcrowded. Cook for 12-15 minutes, turning the skewers halfway through the cooking time. Adjust the time as needed based on the size of your turkey cubes.

Check for Doneness:

Use an instant-read thermometer to ensure the internal temperature of the turkey reaches 165°F (74°C).

Serve and Enjoy:

Once the turkey bites are golden brown and cooked through, remove them from the air fryer. Serve immediately as a delightful appetizer or as part of your Thanksgiving spread.

These air-fried turkey bites with a herb marinade capture the essence of Thanksgiving in every savory bite. The infusion of rosemary, thyme, and sage brings out the richness of the turkey, making this dish a standout addition to your holiday celebrations. Enjoy the crispy exterior and flavorful interior of these delightful turkey bites!

CRISPY SWEET POTATO FRIES WITH CINNAMON SUGAR

Ingredients:

2 large sweet potatoes, peeled and cut into matchsticks or wedges

2 tablespoons cornstarch

2 tablespoons olive oil

1 teaspoon ground cinnamon

2 tablespoons granulated sugar

1/2 teaspoon salt

Cooking spray

Instructions:

Prep the Sweet Potatoes:

Preheat your air fryer to 400°F (200°C) for about 5 minutes.

In a large bowl, toss the sweet potato matchsticks with cornstarch until evenly coated. This helps achieve extra crispiness.

Coat with Olive Oil:

Drizzle olive oil over the sweet potatoes and toss until they are well-coated. The cornstarch and oil combination will contribute to the fries' crisp texture.

Season with Cinnamon Sugar:

In a separate bowl, mix ground cinnamon and granulated sugar. Sprinkle this cinnamon sugar mixture over the sweet potatoes, ensuring an even distribution. Toss to coat.

Arrange in the Air Fryer:

Lightly grease the air fryer basket with cooking spray. Place the sweet potato fries in a single layer, making sure they are not overcrowded to allow for optimal crispiness.

Air Fry the Sweet Potato Fries:

Cook in the preheated air fryer at 400°F (200°C) for 15-18 minutes, shaking the basket or flipping the fries halfway through to ensure even cooking.

Check for Crispiness:

Around the 15-minute mark, check the fries for desired crispiness. You can extend the cooking time if needed, depending on your preferred level of crispiness.

Sprinkle with Salt:

Once the sweet potato fries are done, immediately sprinkle them with salt while they are still hot. This enhances the overall flavor.

Serve and Enjoy:

Transfer the crispy sweet potato fries to a serving dish. Serve them as a delightful side dish or a sweet treat for any occasion.

These crispy sweet potato fries with cinnamon sugar offer a perfect blend of sweetness and crunch. Whether accompanying a holiday meal or enjoyed on their own, these air-fried fries are sure to be a crowd-pleaser. Indulge in the delightful combination of cinnamon, sugar, and the natural sweetness of sweet potatoes!

CHAPTER 3: CHRISTMAS CLASSICS

3.1 Introduction to Christmas Air Fryer Cooking

Capture the festive spirit of Christmas and introduce the joy of using an air fryer for traditional holiday classics.

Set the scene for a Christmas celebration filled with delightful, air-fried creations.

3.2 Festive Air-Fried Ham with Maple Glaze

Dive into the holiday season with a succulent air-fried ham featuring a luscious maple glaze.

Emphasize the efficiency of air frying for achieving a perfect balance of tenderness and flavor.

3.3 Garlic Parmesan Brussels Sprouts

Elevate the classic Brussels sprouts side dish with a garlic parmesan twist, air-fried to golden perfection.

Highlight the simplicity and quick preparation of this savory holiday favorite.

3.4 Cranberry and Brie Stuffed Mushrooms

Introduce an elegant appetizer by combining the richness of brie with the tartness of cranberries, all air-fried for a delightful bite.

Showcase how air frying enhances the textures and flavors of stuffed mushrooms.

3.5 Christmas Morning Cinnamon Rolls

Explore the joy of a Christmas morning tradition with air-fried cinnamon rolls, golden brown and oozing with sweet glaze.

Provide a step-by-step guide for a hassle-free holiday breakfast.

3.6 Peppermint Chocolate Lava Cakes

Delight the senses with individual-sized peppermint chocolate lava cakes, air-fried to perfection.

Share the magic of creating decadent desserts effortlessly with an air fryer.

3.7 Holiday Beverage Pairing: Spiced Apple Cider

Complement the festive dishes with a spiced apple cider recipe, easily prepared in the air fryer.

Offer suggestions for pairing this comforting beverage with the Christmas classics.

3.8 Christmas Table Decor and Presentation Tips

Provide creative ideas for decorating the holiday table to enhance the festive atmosphere.

Share tips on presenting air-fried dishes in an appealing and appetizing manner.

3.9 Reader's Choice: Choose Your Christmas Air-Fried Dish

Engage readers by allowing them to vote on which Christmas air-fried dish they would like featured in an upcoming recipe collection.

Encourage participation and community interaction.

3.10 Conclusion of Chapter 3

Recap the timeless Christmas classics reimagined with the help of an air fryer.

Invite readers to infuse their holiday season with the magic of air-fried creations.

FESTIVE AIR-FRIED HAM WITH MAPLE GLAZE

Ingredients:

1 bone-in ham, fully cooked (about 5-7 pounds)

1 cup pure maple syrup

1/4 cup Dijon mustard

2 tablespoons apple cider vinegar

1 teaspoon ground cinnamon

1/2 teaspoon ground cloves

1/4 teaspoon ground nutmeg

Salt and black pepper, to taste

Fresh rosemary sprigs for garnish (optional)

Instructions:

Preheat the Air Fryer:

Preheat your air fryer to 350°F (180°C) for about 5 minutes.

Prepare the Glaze:

In a small saucepan over medium heat, combine maple syrup, Dijon mustard, apple cider vinegar, ground cinnamon, ground cloves, ground nutmeg, salt, and black pepper. Stir well and simmer for 5-7 minutes until the mixture slightly thickens. Remove from heat and set aside.

Score the Ham:

Using a sharp knife, score the surface of the ham in a diamond pattern. This helps the glaze penetrate and adds a decorative touch.

Apply the Maple Glaze:

Brush a generous amount of the maple glaze over the surface of the ham, ensuring it gets into the scored areas. Reserve some glaze for basting during the air-frying process.

Air Fry the Ham:

Place the glazed ham in the air fryer basket, making sure it fits comfortably. Cook at 350°F (180°C) for 12-15 minutes per pound, basting with the reserved glaze every 15 minutes.

Check for Doneness:

Use a meat thermometer to check the internal temperature of the ham. It should reach at least 140°F (60°C). Adjust cooking time if needed.

Rest and Garnish:

Once done, remove the air-fried ham and let it rest for 10 minutes before carving. Optionally, garnish with fresh rosemary sprigs for a festive touch.

Slice and Serve:

Carve the air-fried ham into slices, drizzling any remaining glaze over the top. Serve warm as the centerpiece of your festive holiday table.

This festive air-fried ham with maple glaze combines the rich flavors of maple, Dijon mustard, and aromatic spices, creating a succulent and impressive holiday main course. The air fryer ensures a beautifully caramelized exterior while keeping the ham moist and flavorful. Enjoy the warmth and festivity of this delightful dish with your loved ones!

GARLIC PARMESAN BRUSSELS SPROUTS

Ingredients:

1 pound Brussels sprouts, trimmed and halved

3 tablespoons olive oil

3 cloves garlic, minced

1/2 cup grated Parmesan cheese

1 teaspoon dried oregano

Salt and black pepper, to taste

Lemon wedges for serving (optional)

Instructions:

Preheat the Air Fryer:

Preheat your air fryer to 375°F (190°C) for about 5 minutes.

Prepare the Brussels Sprouts:

In a bowl, toss the halved Brussels sprouts with olive oil, minced garlic, dried oregano, salt, and black pepper. Ensure the Brussels sprouts are evenly coated with the seasonings.

Air Fry the Brussels Sprouts:

Place the seasoned Brussels sprouts in the air fryer basket, spreading them out for even cooking. Cook at 375°F (190°C) for 15-18 minutes, shaking the basket or tossing the sprouts halfway through.

Check for Crispiness:

Around the 15-minute mark, check the Brussels sprouts for desired crispiness. Extend the cooking time if needed, depending on your preference.

Add Parmesan Cheese:

Sprinkle the grated Parmesan cheese over the Brussels sprouts during the last 5 minutes of cooking. This allows the cheese to melt and create a delicious crust.

Serve and Garnish:

Once the Brussels sprouts are golden brown and crispy, remove them from the air fryer. Transfer to a serving dish and garnish with additional Parmesan if desired. Serve with lemon wedges for a burst of citrusy flavor.

Enjoy as a Flavorful Side:

These garlic Parmesan Brussels sprouts make a fantastic side dish for any occasion. The combination of roasted Brussels sprouts, savory garlic, and nutty Parmesan creates a delightful and flavorful accompaniment to your holiday meals.

These air-fried Brussels sprouts are not only quick and easy to prepare but also bring a burst of flavor to your table. The crispy texture and savory Parmesan coating make them a standout side dish for your festive gatherings. Enjoy the delightful combination of garlic and Parmesan with every bite!

CHAPTER 4: HANUKKAH HIGHLIGHTS

4.1 Introduction to Hanukkah Air Fryer Cooking

Embrace the spirit of Hanukkah and introduce the versatility of air frying for traditional and creative dishes.

Set the stage for a Hanukkah celebration filled with delicious and innovative air-fried delights.

4.2 Air-Fried Latkes with Applesauce

Dive into the holiday with a classic Hanukkah dish— crispy air-fried latkes served with a side of flavorful applesauce.

Emphasize the efficiency of air frying for achieving the perfect latke texture.

4.3 Jelly-Filled Sufganiyot

Explore the sweet side of Hanukkah with air-fried sufganiyot, filled with fruity jelly for a delectable treat.

Share tips on achieving light and fluffy donuts with the air fryer.

4.4 Roasted Vegetable Menorah Platter

Showcase creativity by arranging a menorah-shaped platter featuring a colorful assortment of air-fried roasted vegetables.

Provide ideas for dipping sauces to accompany the vegetable menorah.

4.5 Hanukkah Gelt Chocolate Covered Pretzels

Combine the tradition of Hanukkah gelt with a sweet and salty twist—air-fried chocolate-covered pretzels.

Guide readers through creating a delightful and festive snack.

4.6 Hanukkah Dinner: Air-Fried Chicken Schnitzel

Introduce a Hanukkah dinner favorite—air-fried chicken schnitzel with a crispy golden crust.

Share variations and accompaniments to enhance the schnitzel experience.

4.7 DIY Hanukkah Air-Fried Gift Baskets

Encourage readers to create personalized Hanukkah gift baskets with homemade air-fried treats.

Provide ideas for packaging and including a variety of air-fried goodies.

4.8 Hanukkah Table Decor and Celebration Tips

Offer suggestions for decorating the Hanukkah table and creating a warm and inviting atmosphere.

Provide tips for incorporating traditional symbols into the celebration.

4.9 Reader's Choice: Share Your Hanukkah Air-Fried Creations

Invite readers to share their air-fried Hanukkah creations and traditions.

Highlight a selection of reader submissions to inspire others in celebrating Hanukkah with the air fryer.

4.10 Conclusion of Chapter 4

Recap the Hanukkah highlights presented in the chapter, celebrating the festival of lights with a modern culinary twist.

Extend warm wishes for a joyous and delicious Hanukkah celebration with air-fried delights.

AIR-FRIED LATKES WITH APPLESAUCE

Ingredients:

4 large russet potatoes, peeled

1 large onion, peeled

2 large eggs, beaten

1/4 cup all-purpose flour

1 teaspoon baking powder

Salt and black pepper, to taste

Vegetable oil for brushing

Applesauce for serving

Sour cream (optional, for serving)

Instructions:

Preheat the Air Fryer:

Preheat your air fryer to 400°F (200°C) for about 5 minutes.

Grate Potatoes and Onion:

Grate the peeled potatoes and onion using a box grater or a food processor. Place the grated mixture in a clean kitchen towel and squeeze out excess moisture.

Prepare the Latke Mixture:

In a large bowl, combine the grated potatoes and onion with beaten eggs, all-purpose flour, baking powder, salt, and black pepper. Mix well to form a thick and uniform batter.

Shape Latkes:

Take a portion of the batter and shape it into a flat pancake, squeezing out any excess liquid. Repeat for the remaining batter.

Brush with Oil:

Lightly brush both sides of each latke with vegetable oil. This helps achieve a crispy texture during air frying.

Air Fry the Latkes:

Place the latkes in the air fryer basket, ensuring they are not overcrowded. Cook at 400°F (200°C) for 10-12 minutes, flipping the latkes halfway through the cooking time for even crispiness.

Check for Crispiness:

Around the 10-minute mark, check the latkes for the desired level of crispiness. Extend the cooking time if needed.

Serve with Applesauce:

Once the latkes are golden brown and crispy, remove them from the air fryer. Serve hot with a side of applesauce for dipping. Optionally, offer sour cream as an additional topping.

Enjoy the Crispy Delight:

These air-fried latkes with applesauce are a delightful twist on a Hanukkah classic. Enjoy the crispy exterior and tender interior, perfectly complemented by the sweetness of applesauce.

Air-frying the latkes provides a healthier alternative to traditional frying while maintaining the delicious flavors and textures. Serve these Hanukkah treats as a festive appetizer or side dish, bringing joy to your celebration of the festival of lights!

JELLY-FILLED SUFGANIYOT

Ingredients:

2 1/4 teaspoons (1 packet) active dry yeast

1 cup warm milk

1/4 cup granulated sugar

3 1/2 cups all-purpose flour

1/4 teaspoon salt

1 teaspoon vanilla extract

3 large egg yolks

2 tablespoons unsalted butter, softened

Vegetable oil for frying

Fruit jelly or jam of your choice

Powdered sugar for dusting

Instructions:

Activate the Yeast:

In a bowl, combine warm milk, granulated sugar, and active dry yeast. Let it sit for about 5-10 minutes until frothy.

Prepare the Dough:

In a large mixing bowl, combine the activated yeast mixture with flour, salt, vanilla extract, egg yolks, and softened butter. Mix until a dough forms.

Knead the Dough:

On a floured surface, knead the dough for about 5-7 minutes until it becomes smooth and elastic.

First Rise:

Place the dough in a greased bowl, cover it with a damp cloth, and let it rise in a warm place for 1-1.5 hours or until it has doubled in size.

Roll and Cut the Dough:

Roll out the risen dough to about 1/4-inch thickness. Use a round cookie cutter to cut out circles, approximately 2-3 inches in diameter.

Second Rise:

Place the cut dough circles on a baking sheet, cover them, and let them rise for an additional 30-45 minutes.

Heat the Oil:

In a deep fryer or large, deep pan, heat vegetable oil to 350°F (175°C).

Fry the Sufganiyot:

Carefully place the dough circles in the hot oil, frying each side until golden brown (about 1-2 minutes per side).

Fill with Jelly:

Once the sufganiyot are fried and cooled slightly, use a piping bag or a small tip to fill each sufganiyah with your favorite fruit jelly or jam.

Dust with Powdered Sugar:

Dust the filled sufganiyot with powdered sugar for an extra sweet touch.

Serve and Enjoy:

Serve these delightful jelly-filled sufganiyot as a sweet treat during Hanukkah celebrations. Enjoy the burst of fruity goodness in every bite!

These air-fried jelly-filled sufganiyot offer a delicious twist on a traditional Hanukkah treat. The air fryer ensures a golden exterior and a soft, fluffy interior, making these sweet delights a perfect addition to your festive celebrations.

CHAPTER 5: NEW YEAR'S EVE EATS

5.1 Introduction to New Year's Eve Air Fryer Delights

Ring in the New Year with a collection of scrumptious and hassle-free air-fried dishes.

Introduce the idea of celebrating the countdown with mouthwatering appetizers, snacks, and treats.

5.2 Countdown Calamari Bites with Zesty Dipping Sauce

Kick off the New Year's Eve celebration with crispy air-fried calamari bites, paired with a zesty dipping sauce.

Highlight the simplicity of preparing this restaurant-worthy appetizer at home.

5.3 Truffle Parmesan Fries for a Glamorous Start

Elevate the evening with indulgent truffle parmesan fries, air-fried to perfection.

Showcase how the air fryer can turn a classic into a gourmet New Year's Eve treat.

5.4 Prosciutto-Wrapped Asparagus Spears

Add a touch of elegance to your celebration with air-fried prosciutto-wrapped asparagus spears.

Emphasize the balance of flavors and textures in this stylish appetizer.

5.5 Bubbly Bites: Champagne and Cheese Pairing

Explore the art of pairing champagne with air-fried cheese bites, creating a sophisticated New Year's Eve tasting experience.

Provide suggestions for cheese varieties that complement different champagne flavors.

5.6 Sweet and Spicy Bacon-Wrapped Dates

Delight your taste buds with the contrasting flavors of sweet dates and savory bacon, air-fried for a perfect blend.

Showcase the irresistible combination of sweet, salty, and spicy notes.

5.7 Mini Crab Cakes with Lemon Aioli

Impress your guests with mini crab cakes, air-fried to golden perfection, and served with a refreshing lemon aioli.

Share tips on achieving a crispy exterior and tender crab-filled center.

5.8 New Year's Eve Dessert Platter: Assorted Air-Fried Sweets

Curate a dessert platter featuring an assortment of air-fried sweets, from churros to chocolate-dipped fruit.

Inspire a sweet conclusion to the year with a variety of delectable treats.

5.9 Party Planning Tips for a Memorable New Year's Eve

Offer practical advice on hosting a successful New Year's Eve gathering, including timing tips, decoration ideas, and creating a festive atmosphere.

Encourage readers to embrace the joy of celebrating with friends and family.

5.10 Conclusion of Chapter 5

Recap the enticing New Year's Eve eats presented in the chapter, perfect for welcoming the upcoming year with flavor and flair.

Extend wishes for a joyful celebration and a delicious start to the New Year with air-fried delights.

CHAMPAGNE-INFUSED AIR-FRIED SHRIMP

Ingredients:

1 pound large shrimp, peeled and deveined

1 cup champagne or sparkling wine

2 tablespoons olive oil

3 cloves garlic, minced

1 teaspoon lemon zest

1/2 teaspoon red pepper flakes (adjust to taste)

Salt and black pepper, to taste

Fresh parsley, chopped, for garnish

Lemon wedges, for serving

Instructions:

Marinate the Shrimp:

In a bowl, combine the peeled and deveined shrimp with champagne, olive oil, minced garlic, lemon zest, red pepper flakes, salt, and black pepper. Allow the shrimp to marinate for at least 30 minutes to absorb the flavors.

Preheat the Air Fryer:

Preheat your air fryer to 400°F (200°C) for about 5 minutes.

Prepare the Shrimp for Air Frying:

Remove the shrimp from the marinade, letting any excess liquid drip off. Thread the shrimp onto skewers for easy handling during air frying.

Air Fry the Champagne-Infused Shrimp:

Place the skewered shrimp in the air fryer basket, ensuring they are not overcrowded. Cook at 400°F (200°C) for 6-8 minutes, turning the skewers halfway through for even cooking.

Check for Doneness:

The shrimp should be opaque and cooked through.
Adjust the cooking time based on the size of the shrimp.

Garnish and Serve:

Once the champagne-infused shrimp are cooked,
sprinkle them with freshly chopped parsley for a burst
of color and freshness. Serve hot with lemon wedges on
the side.

Pairing Tip:

Pair these delightful champagne-infused shrimp with a
glass of the same champagne used in the marinade for a
cohesive and sophisticated tasting experience.

Enjoy the Elegance:

Elevate your New Year's Eve celebration with the
luxurious flavors of champagne-infused air-fried shrimp.
The effervescence of champagne adds a subtle
complexity to the shrimp, creating a dish that's perfect
for toasting to the upcoming year.

These shrimp, with a touch of champagne, offer a delightful combination of flavors that will surely impress your guests as you ring in the New Year. Enjoy the elegance and sophistication of this air-fried treat!

CRISPY KALE CHIPS FOR A HEALTHIER SNACK OPTION

Ingredients:

1 bunch of fresh kale, washed and thoroughly dried

1 tablespoon olive oil

1/2 teaspoon garlic powder

1/2 teaspoon onion powder

1/2 teaspoon smoked paprika

Salt, to taste

Instructions:

Preheat the Air Fryer:

Preheat your air fryer to 350°F (175°C) for about 5 minutes.

Prepare the Kale:

Remove the tough stems from the kale leaves and tear the leaves into bite-sized pieces. Ensure the kale is thoroughly dry to achieve maximum crispiness.

Massage with Olive Oil:

In a large bowl, massage the kale pieces with olive oil. Ensure each piece is lightly coated, adding more oil if needed.

Season the Kale:

Sprinkle garlic powder, onion powder, smoked paprika, and salt over the kale. Toss the kale in the bowl to evenly distribute the seasonings.

Air Fry the Kale Chips:

Place the seasoned kale in the air fryer basket, ensuring it's spread out in a single layer for even cooking. You may need to do this in batches depending on the size of your air fryer.

Air Fry for Crispy Perfection:

Air fry at 350°F (175°C) for 5-8 minutes, shaking the basket or tossing the kale halfway through. Keep a close eye to prevent burning, as cooking times may vary.

Check for Crispiness:

The kale chips are done when they are crisp and have a slight golden color. Adjust the cooking time as needed.

Cool and Enjoy:

Allow the kale chips to cool for a few minutes before serving. They will continue to crisp up as they cool. Enjoy as a healthier alternative to traditional snacks!

Crispy kale chips are not only a delicious and crunchy snack but also a nutritious option. Packed with vitamins and minerals, these air-fried kale chips are the perfect guilt-free treat for your New Year's Eve celebration or any occasion. Enjoy the satisfying crunch without compromising on health!

CHAPTER 6: VALENTINE'S DAY DECADENCE

6.1 Introduction to Valentine's Day Air Fryer Delights

Set the stage for a romantic and indulgent Valentine's Day celebration with a selection of decadent air-fried treats.

Introduce the chapter as a guide to creating memorable moments through the art of air-fried culinary delights.

6.2 Love at First Bite: Chocolate-Covered Strawberry Skewers

Kick off the celebration with a romantic twist on a classic—chocolate-covered strawberry skewers, air-fried to perfection.

Highlight the simplicity of preparation and the delightful combination of sweet and juicy flavors.

6.3 Heartfelt Appetizer: Caprese Salad Bites with Balsamic Glaze

Create a savory appetizer with heart-shaped Caprese salad bites, showcasing the elegance of the air fryer.

Explore the harmony of fresh mozzarella, tomatoes, basil, and balsamic glaze.

6.4 Seductive Lobster Tails with Garlic Butter

Elevate the romantic dinner with air-fried lobster tails bathed in garlic butter, a luxurious and impressive dish.

Provide step-by-step instructions for achieving succulent lobster perfection.

6.5 Love Potion: Raspberry-Chocolate Lava Cakes

Dive into the world of romance with individual raspberry-chocolate lava cakes, air-fried for a gooey and decadent center.

Offer tips on achieving the perfect balance of rich chocolate and tart raspberry flavors.

6.6 Aphrodisiac Avocado Fries with Sriracha Aioli

Spice up the celebration with aphrodisiac avocado fries, air-fried and served with a zesty sriracha aioli.

Explore the creamy texture of avocados paired with a kick of heat.

6.7 Romantic Dinner Date: Air-Fried Filet Mignon

Impress your special someone with a romantic dinner featuring air-fried filet mignon, cooked to tender perfection.

Share tips on seasoning and achieving the ideal sear.

6.8 Sweet Endings: Assorted Air-Fried Desserts Platter

Craft a dessert platter featuring an assortment of air-fried treats, from cinnamon sugar donuts to honey-glazed fruit.

Encourage readers to customize their platter for a sweet and personalized ending to the evening.

6.9 Setting the Mood: Valentine's Day Table Decor Tips

Provide inspiration for creating a romantic ambiance with table decor ideas, incorporating themes of love and passion.

Suggest lighting, colors, and decorations to enhance the overall Valentine's Day experience.

6.10 Conclusion of Chapter 6

Recap the luxurious Valentine's Day decadence presented in the chapter, inviting readers to celebrate love through the art of air-fried culinary delights.

Extend warm wishes for a romantic and delicious Valentine's Day celebration filled with love and flavorful moments.

HEART-SHAPED AIR-FRIED CHOCOLATE CHIP COOKIES

Ingredients:

1 cup unsalted butter, softened

1 cup granulated sugar

1 cup packed brown sugar

2 large eggs

1 teaspoon vanilla extract

3 cups all-purpose flour

1 teaspoon baking soda

1/2 teaspoon salt

2 cups chocolate chips

Cooking spray

Instructions:

Preheat the Air Fryer:

Preheat your air fryer to 350°F (175°C) for about 5 minutes.

Prepare the Cookie Dough:

In a large mixing bowl, cream together the softened butter, granulated sugar, and brown sugar until light and fluffy. Add the eggs one at a time, beating well after each addition. Stir in the vanilla extract.

Combine Dry Ingredients:

In a separate bowl, whisk together the flour, baking soda, and salt. Gradually add the dry ingredients to the wet ingredients, mixing until well combined.

Fold in Chocolate Chips:

Gently fold in the chocolate chips until evenly distributed throughout the cookie dough.

Shape the Heart Cookies:

On a floured surface, roll out the cookie dough to about 1/4-inch thickness. Use a heart-shaped cookie cutter to cut out heart-shaped cookies. Place the shaped cookies on a parchment paper-lined tray.

Prep for Air Frying:

Lightly spray the air fryer basket with cooking spray. Arrange the heart-shaped cookies in the air fryer basket, leaving space between each cookie.

Air Fry the Cookies:

Air fry at 350°F (175°C) for 8-10 minutes or until the edges are golden brown. Cooking times may vary, so monitor the cookies closely to prevent over-browning.

Cool and Enjoy:

Once air-fried, carefully transfer the heart-shaped chocolate chip cookies to a wire rack to cool. Allow them to cool completely before serving.

Optional: Drizzle with Chocolate:

For an extra touch, melt some chocolate chips and drizzle it over the cooled cookies. Allow the chocolate drizzle to set before serving.

Serve with Love:

These heart-shaped air-fried chocolate chip cookies are a delightful way to celebrate Valentine's Day. Serve them with love and enjoy the sweet moments with your special someone.

These air-fried chocolate chip cookies, shaped into hearts, are not only adorable but also a delicious way to express love on Valentine's Day or any romantic occasion. Enjoy the warm and gooey chocolate chips in every heart-shaped bite!

ROMANTIC DINNER IDEAS USING THE AIR FRYER.

Romantic Air-Fried Dinner Ideas

Air-Fried Lobster Tails with Garlic Butter:

Impress your date with succulent lobster tails air-fried to perfection. Drizzle with garlic butter for a luxurious touch. Serve with a side of roasted vegetables or a light salad.

Filet Mignon for Two:

Create an intimate dinner with air-fried filet mignon. Seasoned with your favorite herbs and spices, these tender steaks cook quickly in the air fryer. Pair them with a red wine reduction sauce for added elegance.

Heart-Shaped Chicken Parmesan:

Shape chicken breasts into hearts, bread them with a flavorful coating, and air fry until golden and crispy. Top with marinara sauce and melted mozzarella for a romantic twist on classic chicken Parmesan.

Stuffed Bell Peppers with Quinoa and Veggies:

Prepare heart-shaped stuffed bell peppers filled with a mixture of quinoa, veggies, and your choice of protein. Air fry until the peppers are tender, creating a visually appealing and healthy dinner.

Salmon en Papillote with Lemon and Dill:

Seal seasoned salmon fillets, lemon slices, and fresh dill in parchment paper parcels. Air fry for a quick and elegant "en papillote" dish. The result is moist and flavorful salmon with minimal effort.

Coconut Shrimp for Two:

Create a tropical and romantic vibe with air-fried coconut shrimp. The crispy coconut coating pairs perfectly with a sweet and tangy dipping sauce. Serve with a side of mango salsa for a burst of freshness.

Balsamic Glazed Chicken Thighs:

Marinate chicken thighs in a balsamic glaze and air fry until caramelized and juicy. The sweet and tangy flavors make this dish sophisticated yet simple to prepare.

Caprese-Stuffed Portobello Mushrooms:

Elevate your dinner with portobello mushrooms stuffed with mozzarella, tomatoes, and fresh basil. Air fry until the cheese is melted and bubbly. Drizzle with balsamic glaze for an extra layer of flavor.

Air-Fried Ravioli with Pesto Cream Sauce:

Serve heart-shaped or regular ravioli air-fried until golden and crispy. Prepare a creamy pesto sauce to accompany the ravioli, creating a comforting and romantic pasta dish.

Chocolate-Covered Strawberry Skewers:

End the evening with a sweet treat. Skewer strawberries and air-fry until they develop a slight crispness. Dip them in melted chocolate for a decadent and shareable dessert.

Pair these air-fried romantic dinner ideas with your favorite wine, set a beautifully decorated table, and enjoy a delightful evening with your loved one.

CHAPTER 7: EASTER EXTRAVAGANZA

7.1 Introduction to Easter Air Fryer Delights

Welcome the joyous season of Easter with a delightful array of air-fried recipes that elevate traditional favorites.

Emphasize the convenience and creativity the air fryer brings to Easter cooking.

7.2 Eggcellent Appetizers: Deviled Eggs Three Ways

Kick off the Easter celebration with creative variations of deviled eggs, air-fried to perfection.

Explore different flavor profiles, from classic to spicy or herb-infused, to suit every palate.

7.3 Air-Fried Carrot Fritters with Yogurt Dipping Sauce

Showcase the versatility of carrots in a flavorful and crispy form—air-fried carrot fritters served with a refreshing yogurt dipping sauce.

Highlight the use of seasonal produce for a vibrant appetizer.

7.4 Rosemary Garlic Lamb Chops with Mint Chimichurri

Elevate the Easter feast with succulent rosemary garlic lamb chops, air-fried to achieve a perfect crust. Serve with a zesty mint chimichurri for a burst of freshness.

7.5 Spring Vegetable Medley: Air-Fried Asparagus and Snap Peas

Create a vibrant side dish with air-fried asparagus and snap peas. Seasoned with herbs and lemon, this medley celebrates the flavors of spring.

7.6 Spinach and Feta Stuffed Chicken Breasts

Present an elegant main course with air-fried spinach and feta-stuffed chicken breasts. The air fryer ensures a crispy exterior while keeping the filling moist and flavorful.

7.7 Honey Glazed Ham with Pineapple Rings

Make the centerpiece of your Easter table a glazed ham with a touch of honey sweetness. Air fry for a caramelized exterior and juicy interior, garnished with pineapple rings for a tropical twist.

7.8 Easter Egg-Shaped Bread Rolls

Delight your guests with Easter egg-shaped bread rolls, air-fried to golden perfection. These adorable rolls add a festive touch to the dinner table.

7.9 Festive Air-Fried Dessert Platter: Hot Cross Buns and Carrot Cake Bites

Create a dessert platter featuring air-fried hot cross buns and carrot cake bites. These sweet treats capture the essence of Easter with delightful flavors.

7.10 Easter Egg Hunt-Inspired Treats for Kids

Engage the little ones with air-fried treats inspired by Easter egg hunts. Share playful recipes like air-fried egg-shaped cookies and bunny-shaped snacks.

7.11 Decorative Easter Table Setting Ideas

Offer inspiration for a beautiful Easter table with decorative ideas, from floral centerpieces to themed place settings.

Encourage readers to add a touch of creativity to their Easter gatherings.

7.12 Conclusion of Chapter 7

Summarize the Easter extravaganza presented in the chapter, encouraging readers to embrace the joy of the season with delicious and air-fried delights.

Extend warm wishes for a festive and memorable Easter celebration filled with culinary delights.

HONEY GLAZED AIR-FRIED HAM

Ingredients:

1 bone-in ham, pre-cooked and fully cooked (around 5-7 pounds)

1/2 cup honey

1/4 cup Dijon mustard

1/4 cup brown sugar

2 tablespoons apple cider vinegar

1 teaspoon ground cloves (optional, for added flavor)

Whole cloves for garnish (optional)

Pineapple rings for garnish (optional)

Instructions:

Preheat the Air Fryer:

Preheat your air fryer to 350°F (175°C) for about 5 minutes.

Prepare the Glaze:

In a small saucepan, combine honey, Dijon mustard, brown sugar, apple cider vinegar, and ground cloves. Heat over medium heat, stirring constantly, until the mixture is well combined and slightly thickened. Remove from heat and set aside.

Score the Ham:

Using a sharp knife, score the surface of the ham in a diamond pattern. If desired, insert whole cloves into the center of each diamond for added flavor.

Brush with Glaze:

Brush the prepared honey glaze generously over the surface of the ham, ensuring it gets into the scored areas for maximum flavor.

Air Fry the Glazed Ham:

Place the glazed ham in the air fryer basket, making sure it's not touching the sides for even cooking. Cook at 350°F (175°C) for approximately 12-15 minutes per pound, brushing the ham with additional glaze every 20-30 minutes.

Check for Doneness:

Use a meat thermometer to check the internal temperature of the ham. It should reach at least 140°F (60°C). Adjust the cooking time if needed.

Garnish (Optional):

If desired, garnish the ham with pineapple rings during the last 10-15 minutes of cooking for a decorative touch.

Rest and Serve:

Once the ham reaches the desired temperature, remove it from the air fryer. Allow it to rest for a few minutes before slicing.

Slice and Enjoy:

Slice the honey glazed air-fried ham into portions and serve warm. Spoon any remaining glaze from the air fryer basket over the slices for an extra burst of flavor.

This honey glazed air-fried ham is a delicious centerpiece for your Easter feast or any special occasion. The air fryer ensures a caramelized exterior while keeping the ham moist and flavorful. Enjoy the sweet and savory goodness of this classic dish!

EASTER EGG-SHAPED MOZZARELLA BITES

Ingredients:

1 package (approx. 8 ounces) mini mozzarella balls (pearl size)

1 cup all-purpose flour

2 large eggs, beaten

1 cup breadcrumbs (seasoned, for added flavor)

Cooking spray

Instructions:

Prepare the Mozzarella Balls:

Drain the mini mozzarella balls if they are packed in liquid. Pat them dry with a paper towel to remove excess moisture.

Set Up the Breading Station:

Create a breading station with three bowls. Place flour in the first bowl, beaten eggs in the second bowl, and breadcrumbs in the third bowl.

Coat Mozzarella Balls:

Roll each mozzarella ball in the flour, shaking off any excess. Dip it into the beaten eggs, ensuring it's well-coated. Roll it in breadcrumbs, pressing gently to adhere the breadcrumbs to the surface.

Shape into Easter Eggs:

Using your hands, shape the breaded mozzarella balls into egg shapes. Press and mold them gently to achieve the desired Easter egg shape. Place them on a plate or tray.

Chill (Optional):

For better results, you can refrigerate the shaped mozzarella bites for about 15-20 minutes. This helps the coating set and adhere well during air frying.

Preheat the Air Fryer:

Preheat your air fryer to 375°F (190°C) for about 5 minutes.

Air Fry the Mozzarella Bites:

Lightly coat the air fryer basket with cooking spray. Place the shaped mozzarella bites in the basket, ensuring they are not touching each other. Air fry for 5-7 minutes or until golden and crispy.

Check for Crispiness:

Keep an eye on the mozzarella bites and adjust the cooking time if needed. The goal is to achieve a golden and crispy exterior while ensuring the cheese inside remains gooey.

Serve Warm:

Once air-fried, transfer the Easter egg-shaped mozzarella bites to a serving plate. Serve them warm with your favorite dipping sauce.

Dipping Sauce Ideas:

Consider serving these mozzarella bites with marinara sauce, pesto, or a balsamic glaze for dipping.

These Easter egg-shaped mozzarella bites are a fun and festive addition to your Easter gathering. The air fryer ensures a crispy coating with a gooey, melted mozzarella center. Enjoy these delightful bites as a playful appetizer or snack during your Easter celebration!

CHAPTER 8: FOURTH OF JULY FAVORITES

8.1 Introduction to Fourth of July Air Fryer Delights

Dive into the patriotic spirit with a collection of air-fried recipes perfect for celebrating Independence Day.

Highlight the versatility of the air fryer for creating delicious and crowd-pleasing dishes.

8.2 Red, White, and Blueberry Caprese Skewers

Kick off your Fourth of July celebration with vibrant caprese skewers featuring fresh mozzarella, cherry tomatoes, and blueberries. Drizzle with balsamic glaze for added flavor.

8.3 All-American Air-Fried Buffalo Chicken Wings

Serve up a classic favorite with air-fried buffalo chicken wings. These crispy and spicy wings are sure to be a hit at your Fourth of July gathering.

8.4 Grilled Corn on the Cob with Chili-Lime Butter

Elevate traditional corn on the cob by air-frying it with a flavorful chili-lime butter. The air fryer adds a smoky touch to this Independence Day staple.

8.5 Patriotic Pesto Pasta Salad

Create a colorful and flavorful pasta salad using red and blue pasta shapes, cherry tomatoes, and feta cheese. Toss it in a vibrant pesto dressing for a festive side dish.

8.6 Firecracker Shrimp Tacos with Avocado Crema

Spice up your Fourth of July menu with air-fried firecracker shrimp tacos. Top them with a cool and creamy avocado crema for a perfect balance of flavors.

8.7 Star-Spangled Sweet Potato Fries

Cut sweet potatoes into star shapes and air-fry them until golden and crispy. These star-spangled sweet potato fries make for a patriotic and delicious side dish.

8.8 Grilled Watermelon Skewers with Mint-Lime Drizzle

Refresh your guests with air-fried grilled watermelon skewers. Drizzle with a mint-lime sauce for a unique and hydrating treat on a hot Fourth of July day.

8.9 American Flag Fruit Pizza

Craft a dessert centerpiece with an American flag fruit pizza. Use a sugar cookie crust, cream cheese frosting, and arrange strawberries and blueberries to resemble the U.S. flag.

8.10 Independence Day Ice Cream Sandwiches

- Assemble festive ice cream sandwiches using red and blue cookies or food coloring. Sandwich your favorite ice cream between these patriotic cookies for a cool and sweet treat.

8.11 Sparkling Lemonade Spritzers

- Quench the thirst of your guests with refreshing sparkling lemonade spritzers. Add red and blue berries for a patriotic twist and serve in clear cups for a visually appealing drink.

8.12 Fireworks Show Snack Mix

- Create a snack mix with red and blue candies, popcorn, and pretzels. Package it in individual servings for guests to enjoy during the Fourth of July fireworks show.

8.13 Conclusion of Chapter 8

- Summarize the Fourth of July favorites presented in the chapter, offering readers a variety of air-fried dishes to elevate their Independence Day celebrations.

- Wish readers a joyful and delicious Fourth of July filled with good food, great company, and patriotic spirit.

BBQ CHICKEN WINGS WITH A SMOKY RUB.

Smoky BBQ Chicken Wings

Ingredients:

2 pounds chicken wings, split at joints, tips discarded

2 tablespoons smoked paprika

1 tablespoon brown sugar

1 teaspoon garlic powder

1 teaspoon onion powder

1 teaspoon cumin

1/2 teaspoon cayenne pepper (adjust to taste for spice)

Salt and black pepper, to taste

2 tablespoons olive oil

BBQ sauce for glazing (optional)

Fresh cilantro or parsley, chopped, for garnish

Instructions:

Prepare the Chicken Wings:

Pat the chicken wings dry with paper towels to remove excess moisture. Place them in a large bowl.

Create the Smoky Rub:

In a small bowl, mix together smoked paprika, brown sugar, garlic powder, onion powder, cumin, cayenne pepper, salt, and black pepper to create the smoky rub.

Coat the Wings:

Drizzle the chicken wings with olive oil and toss to coat evenly. Sprinkle the smoky rub over the wings, ensuring they are well-covered. Massage the rub into the wings for even flavor distribution.

Marinate (Optional):

For intensified flavor, cover the bowl and let the wings marinate in the refrigerator for at least 30 minutes or up to overnight.

Preheat the Air Fryer:

Preheat your air fryer to 400°F (200°C) for about 5 minutes.

Air Fry the Wings:

Place the seasoned chicken wings in the air fryer basket, ensuring they are not overcrowded. Cook at 400°F (200°C) for 25-30 minutes, flipping the wings halfway through for even cooking. Adjust the time based on your air fryer and the size of the wings.

Check for Crispiness:

The wings should be golden brown and crispy. If you desire an extra layer of flavor, brush the wings with BBQ sauce during the last 5 minutes of cooking.

Garnish and Serve:

Once air-fried, transfer the smoky BBQ chicken wings to a serving platter. Garnish with chopped cilantro or parsley for freshness.

Dipping Sauce (Optional):

Serve the wings with your favorite dipping sauce or additional BBQ sauce on the side.

Enjoy the Smoky Goodness:

These air-fried smoky BBQ chicken wings are bursting with flavor. Enjoy them as a crowd-pleasing appetizer or as a main course for your barbecue-themed meal.

Perfect for any occasion, especially Fourth of July celebrations!

Note: Cooking times may vary depending on the size and type of air fryer. Always check the internal temperature of the wings, ensuring it reaches at least 165°F (74°C) for safe consumption.

PATRIOTIC AIR-FRIED DESSERTS FOR INDEPENDENCE DAY

Red, White, and Blue Air-Fried Donuts:

Prepare donut dough and shape them into rings. Air fry until golden, then dip in red and blue glazes made with food coloring. Finish with white icing and patriotic sprinkles.

Star-Spangled Air-Fried Apple Pies:

Cut puff pastry into star shapes, fill with apple pie filling, and air-fry until golden brown. Drizzle with red and blue icing for a festive touch.

Independence Day Air-Fried Churros:

Pipe churro dough into star shapes, air-fry until crispy, and roll them in a mix of cinnamon and sugar. Serve with red and blueberry dipping sauces.

Patriotic Air-Fried Cheesecake Bites:

Cut cheesecake into bite-sized pieces, dip in white chocolate, and decorate with red and blue edible glitter or sprinkles. Air-fry briefly to set the coating.

Fourth of July Air-Fried Fruit Kabobs:

Skewer red strawberries, white marshmallows, and blueberries onto sticks. Air-fry briefly to slightly caramelize the fruit. Serve with a yogurt dip.

American Flag Air-Fried Pound Cake:

Cut pound cake into squares, arranging them to resemble the American flag on a serving tray. Use blueberries for the stars and raspberries and white icing for the stripes.

Red, White, and Blue Air-Fried Cannoli Cones:

Fill mini cannoli shells with a mixture of mascarpone, powdered sugar, and vanilla. Dip the ends in red and blue sprinkles. Air-fry briefly for a crunchy texture.

Patriotic Air-Fried Brownie Bites:

Bake brownie batter in mini muffin cups, top with whipped cream or frosting, and garnish with a mix of red and blue berries. Air-fry for a warm and gooey finish.

Firecracker Air-Fried Popcorn Balls:

Create popcorn balls with a mix of red, white, and blue candies. Form them into firecracker shapes and air-fry briefly for a crunchy coating.

Star-Spangled Air-Fried Shortcakes:

Cut shortcakes into star shapes, air-fry until golden, and assemble with layers of whipped cream and fresh strawberries and blueberries. Drizzle with a berry sauce.

Patriotic Air-Fried Rice Krispie Treats:

Make Rice Krispie treats, cut them into squares, and dip the edges in red and blue icing. Decorate with white chocolate drizzle for a festive look.

Independence Day Air-Fried S'mores:

Assemble s'mores with red and blue marshmallows. Air-fry briefly to melt the chocolate and marshmallows. Serve with graham crackers.

These patriotic air-fried desserts are not only delicious but also add a festive touch to your Independence Day celebration. Get creative with colors, shapes, and decorations to make them stand out at your Fourth of July gathering!

CHAPTER 9: TIPS FOR ADAPTING RECIPES

9.1 Introduction to Recipe Adaptations

Explore the art of culinary creativity by adapting recipes to suit individual preferences, dietary needs, or ingredient availability.

Emphasize the importance of understanding the fundamentals of a dish before making modifications.

9.2 Understanding Flavor Profiles

Delve into the essential elements of flavor profiles, discussing the balance of sweet, salty, sour, and savory notes.

Provide tips on adjusting seasonings to achieve the desired taste in adapted recipes.

9.3 Ingredient Substitutions

Guide readers on making informed ingredient substitutions based on dietary restrictions, allergies, or pantry availability.

Highlight common ingredient alternatives and their impact on the final dish.

9.4 Customizing Texture and Consistency

Explore methods for adjusting the texture and consistency of dishes, such as thickening sauces, varying cooking times, or experimenting with alternative cooking methods.

Provide examples of how modifying these elements can enhance the overall dining experience.

9.5 Tailoring Recipes for Dietary Preferences

Address common dietary preferences and restrictions, including vegetarian, vegan, gluten-free, and low-carb options.

Offer practical tips for adapting recipes to meet specific dietary needs while preserving flavor and satisfaction.

9.6 Scaling Recipes for Crowds or Solo Dining

Discuss strategies for scaling recipes to accommodate different serving sizes, whether cooking for a large gathering or preparing a meal for one.

Provide guidance on adjusting ingredient quantities and cooking times accordingly.

9.7 Enhancing Nutritional Value

Explore ways to boost the nutritional content of recipes by incorporating nutrient-dense ingredients, reducing added sugars, or increasing fiber content.

Share insights on maintaining a balance between taste and nutritional benefits.

9.8 Balancing Heat and Spice

Dive into the world of heat and spice, discussing techniques for adjusting spiciness levels to suit individual preferences.

Offer advice on incorporating spices and peppers gradually to achieve the desired level of heat.

9.9 Experimenting with Global Flavors

Encourage readers to explore global cuisines by adapting recipes to incorporate diverse flavors, herbs, and spices.

Provide a guide to understanding the flavor profiles of different cuisines and adapting them creatively.

9.10 Recording Adaptations and Learnings

Stress the importance of keeping notes on recipe adaptations, recording successful modifications, and learning from experiments.

Share the value of personalizing recipes and creating a culinary repertoire.

9.11 Encouragement for Culinary Creativity

Conclude the chapter by encouraging readers to embrace culinary creativity and view recipes as starting points for their own culinary expressions.

Remind them that adapting recipes is a journey of discovery and personalization.

9.12 Conclusion of Chapter 9

Summarize the key tips and insights provided in the chapter, reinforcing the idea that adapting recipes is a skill that enhances one's cooking experience.

Encourage readers to experiment, trust their instincts, and enjoy the process of making each dish uniquely their own.

GUIDELINES FOR ADJUSTING PORTION SIZES FOR DIFFERENT CELEBRATIONS.

Adjusting Portion Sizes for Different Celebrations

Consider the Occasion:

Tailor portion sizes based on the nature of the celebration. For casual gatherings, slightly larger portions might be suitable, while more formal events may benefit from smaller, refined servings.

Guest Count Matters:

Calculate the number of guests and adjust portion sizes accordingly. Larger gatherings may allow for smaller individual portions, while intimate dinners call for more generous servings.

Diversify the Menu:

If serving a variety of dishes, ensure each portion is modest to allow guests to enjoy a range of flavors. For smaller gatherings, consider featuring fewer dishes with larger portions for a more indulgent experience.

Balancing Appetizers and Main Courses:

For events with numerous appetizers, reduce main course portions to avoid overwhelming guests. Conversely, for a dinner-centric celebration, provide more substantial main course servings.

Buffet-style Considerations:

For buffet-style settings, offer smaller portions of each dish to allow guests to sample a variety. Ensure there's an ample quantity of each item to accommodate multiple servings.

Scaling Dessert Portions:

Dessert portions can vary based on the number of courses and the richness of the offerings. In multi-course meals, opt for smaller dessert portions, while standalone dessert events may feature more substantial servings.

Age and Preferences:

Consider the age and preferences of your guests. Children may prefer smaller portions, while adults may enjoy larger servings. Tailor portions to accommodate diverse tastes and dietary needs.

Cultural and Regional Considerations:

Be mindful of cultural norms and regional expectations regarding portion sizes. Some cultures may appreciate more substantial servings, while others prefer a variety of smaller portions.

Account for Dietary Preferences:

If dietary preferences or restrictions are known, adjust portion sizes accordingly. For example, vegetarian or vegan options might have larger portions to compensate for fewer protein-rich elements.

Balance Hearty and Light Options:

Achieve a balance between hearty and lighter options in the menu. Ensure that guests have a satisfying meal without feeling overly full, allowing them to enjoy the celebration without discomfort.

Utilize Individual Servings:

Consider using individual servings for certain dishes, especially desserts or appetizers. This not only enhances presentation but also facilitates portion control.

Encourage Seconds:

For more casual celebrations, consider providing slightly smaller portions with the option for guests to have seconds. This allows them to customize their meal based on appetite and preferences.

Seasonal and Ingredient Availability:

Factor in seasonal availability of ingredients. Adjust portion sizes for dishes featuring seasonal produce or special ingredients, ensuring they are highlighted without excess.

Test and Adjust:

If uncertain, test portion sizes during a trial run or smaller gathering to gauge guest feedback. Adjust based on their preferences and the overall atmosphere of the celebration.

Consider Leftovers:

Account for the potential of leftovers, especially for dishes that age well. Adjust portion sizes to minimize food waste while allowing guests to enjoy the celebration.

By keeping these guidelines in mind, you can adapt portion sizes to suit the specific dynamics and atmosphere of different celebrations, ensuring that guests enjoy a well-balanced and satisfying dining experience.

SUGGESTIONS FOR INCORPORATING DIETARY PREFERENCES (E.G., VEGETARIAN, GLUTEN-FREE).

Incorporating Dietary Preferences in Menus

Diverse Menu Options:

Offer a diverse range of menu items to cater to various dietary preferences. Include options for vegetarians, vegans, gluten-free, and other common dietary needs.

Clear Labeling:

Clearly label dishes to indicate their suitability for specific dietary preferences. This helps guests quickly identify options that align with their dietary needs.

Vegetarian Appetizers:

Start the meal with vegetarian appetizers such as stuffed mushrooms, bruschetta with tomatoes and basil, or vegetable spring rolls. These options appeal to a broad audience.

Gluten-Free Grains:

Incorporate gluten-free grains like quinoa or rice into main courses. This provides a hearty base that accommodates gluten-free and vegetarian diets.

Protein Alternatives:

Offer protein alternatives such as tofu, tempeh, or plant-based meat substitutes to cater to vegetarian and vegan guests. These can be incorporated into various dishes like stir-fries, tacos, or pasta.

Customizable Salad Bar:

Set up a customizable salad bar with a variety of fresh vegetables, fruits, nuts, seeds, and protein options. This allows guests to create salads that align with their dietary preferences.

Gluten-Free Breads and Crackers:

Include gluten-free bread or crackers as part of appetizer spreads. This ensures that guests with gluten sensitivities can enjoy the communal aspects of the meal.

Alternative Pasta Options:

Offer gluten-free pasta as an alternative to traditional wheat-based pasta. Create pasta dishes with gluten-free sauces and ingredients.

Vegetarian Main Courses:

Showcase hearty vegetarian main courses like stuffed bell peppers, vegetable lasagna, or eggplant Parmesan. Ensure these dishes are flavorful and satisfying.

Dairy-Free Desserts:

Include dairy-free dessert options like fruit sorbets, coconut milk-based ice creams, or flourless chocolate cakes. These options appeal to both lactose-intolerant and vegan guests.

Plant-Based Side Dishes:

Feature plant-based side dishes such as roasted vegetables, quinoa salads, or sautéed greens. These can complement a variety of main courses and accommodate different dietary preferences.

Allergen-Free Stations:

Consider setting up allergen-free stations that clearly indicate the absence of specific allergens like gluten, dairy, or nuts. This provides a safe and enjoyable dining experience for guests with allergies.

Communication with Guests:

Prior to the event, communicate with guests to understand their dietary preferences and restrictions. This allows for better planning and ensures everyone feels accommodated.

Flexibility in Recipes:

Choose recipes that can easily accommodate substitutions. For instance, using gluten-free flour or dairy alternatives in recipes without compromising taste.

Educate Staff:

Ensure that the kitchen and serving staff are educated on various dietary preferences and allergies. This helps in preventing cross-contamination and addressing guest inquiries accurately.

By incorporating these suggestions, you create a thoughtful and inclusive menu that caters to a diverse range of dietary preferences, allowing all guests to enjoy the celebration without compromise.

CONCLUSION

In the journey through this culinary exploration, we've embarked on a flavorful adventure that embraces creativity, adaptation, and inclusivity in the kitchen. From crafting holiday air fryer extravaganzas to tailoring recipes for diverse celebrations, we've delved into the art of culinary expression.

In the spirit of adaptability, we learned the importance of adjusting portion sizes based on occasions, accommodating dietary preferences, and fostering a sense of inclusiveness around the dining table. The tips for adapting recipes served as a compass, guiding us to experiment, innovate, and make each dish uniquely our own.

Whether crafting heartwarming Thanksgiving delights, sizzling Fourth of July favorites, or patriotic air-fried desserts for Independence Day, the recipes shared aimed to inspire and elevate celebrations. From the smoky aroma of BBQ chicken wings to the sweet indulgence of air-fried donuts, each dish added its own distinctive note to the symphony of flavors.

As we explored the nuances of adjusting recipes for different celebrations, we recognized that the kitchen is a canvas where culinary preferences, dietary needs, and creative expressions harmonize. From understanding flavor profiles to incorporating diverse ingredients, the guidelines provided were tools for crafting culinary masterpieces.

In the final chapter, we embraced the freedom to adapt recipes with finesse, understanding that the joy of cooking lies not just in following instructions but in making them uniquely ours. The encouragement to record learnings, experiment with global flavors, and view recipes as starting points became the anthem of our culinary journey.

In conclusion, the kitchen is more than a space for preparing meals; it's a realm of creativity, connection, and celebration. As you continue your culinary exploration, may these insights and recipes serve as companions, inspiring you to infuse every dish with your unique flair and passion. Whether it's a holiday feast, a casual gathering, or a quiet dinner for two, may your culinary adventures be filled with joy, flavor, and the warmth of shared moments around the table. Happy cooking!

Printed in Great Britain
by Amazon

37608392R10066